# HELLO BIRD.

BY LESLIE FALCONER

ILLUSTRATED BY KELLY NOGOSKI

First published by Experience Early Learning Company
7243 Scotchwood Lane, Grawn, Michigan 49637 USA

Copyright © 2019 by Experience Early Learning Co.
Manufactured in No. 8, Yin Li Street, Tian He District, Guangzhou,
Guangdong, China by Sun Fly Printing Limited
3rd Printing 01/2022

ISBN 978-1-937954-13-0
Visit us at www.ExperienceEarlyLearning.com

# HELLO BIRD.
# WHY ARE YOU SO STILL?

TICKLE THE ROBIN'S RED BREAST,
THEN TURN THE PAGE AND LOOK IN THE NEST.

LITTLE BLUE EGGS—
ARE THEY NEW?
HOW MANY?
ONE, TWO.

# HELLO BIRD.
# HOW MANY ARE INSIDE?

KNOCK ON THE COOP ... ONE, TWO, THREE, FOUR.
NOW TURN THE PAGE TO SEE SOME MORE.

# MORE CHICKENS
## COME OUT TO FEED.

TRY TO PECK THE YELLOW SEED.

# HELLO BIRD.
# WHERE DID YOU GO?

PAT PAT PAT WITH YOUR HAND,
THE SMALLEST FOOTPRINTS IN THE SAND.

10

11

# HELLO SANDPIPER.
# NOW I SEE
# YOU ARE IN THE GRASS
# HIDING FROM ME.

# HELLO BIRD.
# WHAT MAKES YOU SCARED?

STOMP STOMP STOMP ON THE GROUND,
SHAKE THE BOOK WITH A THUNDERING SOUND.

# OH, A STORM,
# BUT YOU'RE NOT SHY.

TRY TO COUNT THE PEACOCK EYES.

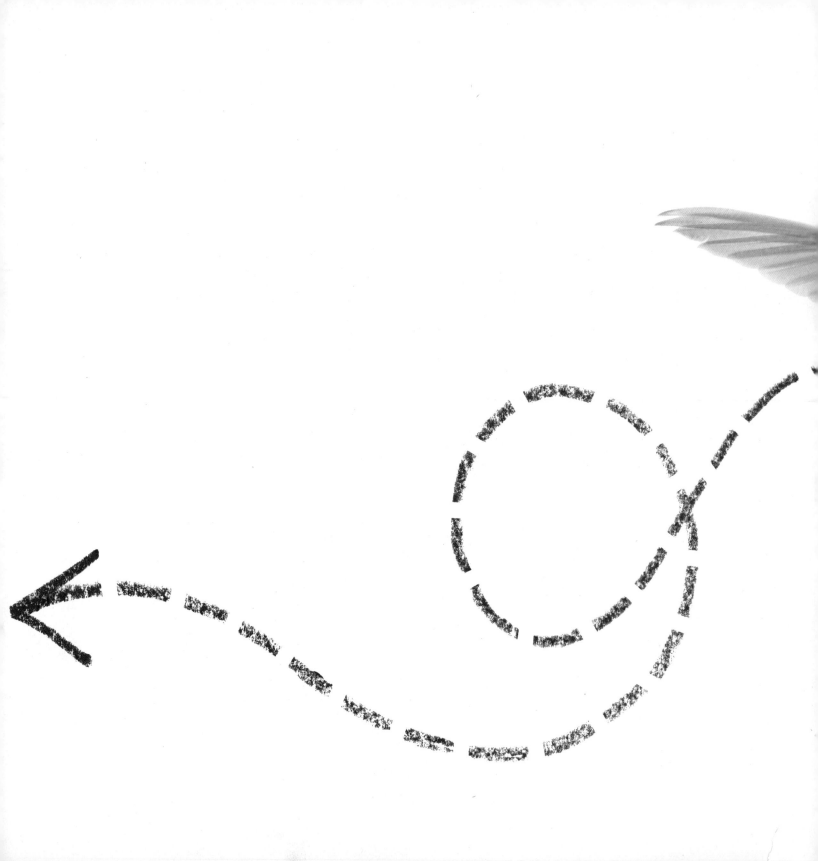

# HELLO BIRD.

# WHERE DO YOU FLY?

TURN THE PAGES BACK TO ONE,
THEN FORWARD TO THE SHINING SUN.

FORWARD, BACKWARD,
UP AND DOWN,
THE HUMMINGBIRD
ZIPS ROUND AND ROUND.

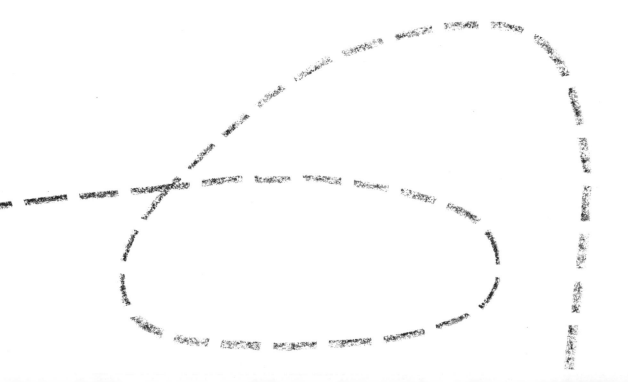

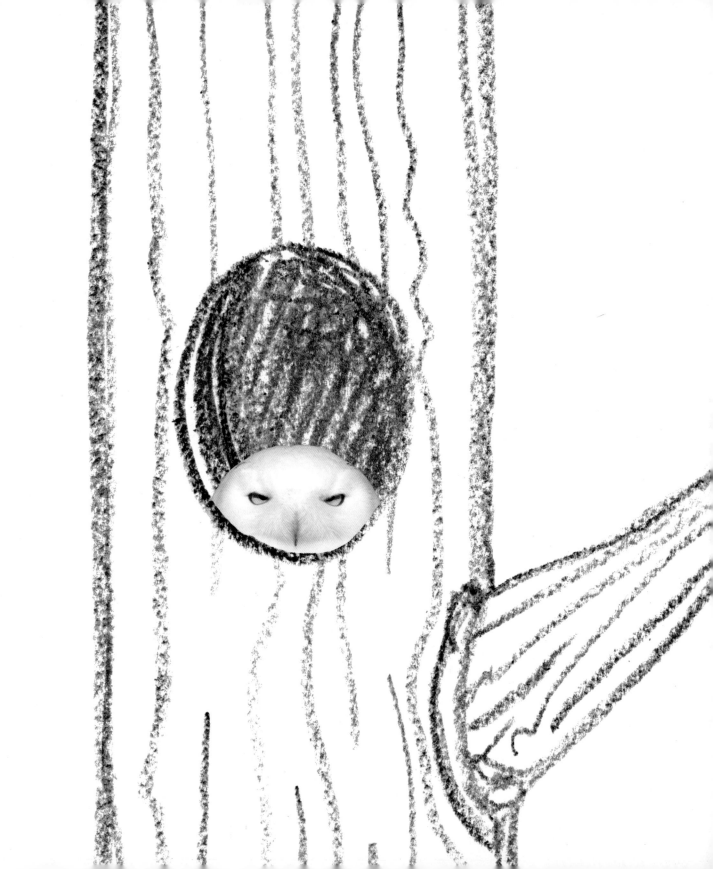

# HELLO BIRD.
# WHO, WHO ARE YOU?

KNOCK ON THE TREE. NOT TOO LOUD, QUIETLY.

# SNOWY OWL!
# YOU'RE CAMOUFLAGED
# FROM SIGHT.

HIDE THIS BOOK BEHIND SOMETHING WHITE.

# HELLO BIRDS.
# WHO LIKES THE COLD?

TAP THE BLUEBIRD WITH YOUR ELBOW
AND THE RED BIRD WITH YOUR TOE.
THEN TURN THE PAGE TO SEE
WHO'S STANDING IN THE SNOW.

# A CARDINAL LOVES THE COLD, I'M TOLD!

CAN YOU COUNT SNOWFLAKES UP TO 10,
THEN START THE BOOK AND READ AGAIN?

# MORE WORDS ON BIRDS!

A **PEACOCK** IS A MALE AND A PEAHEN IS A FEMALE. BABY PEAFOWL ARE CALLED PEACHICKS.

**SANDPIPERS** CAN LIVE TO BE UP TO 12 YEARS OLD. THEY HAVE LONG LEGS THAT HELP THEM RUN.

AN **OWL** HAS THREE EYELIDS: ONE FOR BLINKING, ONE FOR SLEEPING AND ONE FOR KEEPING THE EYE CLEAN AND HEALTHY.

THE **CHICKEN** IS THE CLOSEST LIVING RELATIVE OF THE T-REX.

**HUMMINGBIRDS** CAN FLY IN MANY DIRECTIONS, INCLUDING BACKWARD!

AN **AMERICAN ROBIN'S** EGGS ARE ABOUT THE SIZE OF A QUARTER AND ARE LIGHT BLUE.

THE **NORTHERN CARDINAL** CAN ADAPT TO MANY CLIMATES AND DOESN'T MIGRATE, SO YOU CAN SPOT THEM IN THE WINTER!

THE END